The Thomas Jefferson Memorial

Ted and Lola Schaefer

Heinemann Library
Chicago, Illinois

© 2006 Heinemann Library
a division of Reed Elsevier Inc.
Chicago, Illinois

Customer Service 888-454-2279

Visit our website at www.heinemannlibrary.com

Designed by Richard Parker and Mike Hogg Design
Illustrations by Jeff Edwards
Originated by Chroma Graphics (Overseas) Pte.Ltd
Printed and bound in China by South China Printing Company

10 09 08 07 06
10 9 8 7 6 5 4 3 2 1

Library of Congress Cataloging-in-Publication Data
Schaefer, Ted, 1948-
  The Thomas Jefferson Memorial / Ted and Lola M. Schaefer.
    p. cm. -- (Symbols of freedom)
  Includes index.
  ISBN 1-4034-6660-2 (library binding-hardcover) -- ISBN 1-4034-6669-6 (pbk.)
  1. Thomas Jefferson Memorial (Washington, D.C.)--Juvenile literature. 2. Jefferson, Thomas, 1743-1826--Monuments--Washington (D.C.)--Juvenile literature. 3. Washington (D.C.)--Buildings, structures, etc.--Juvenile literature. I. Schaefer, Lola M., 1950- II. Title. III. Series.
  F203.4.J4S33 2005
  975.3--dc22

                            2005002038

Acknowledgments
The publishers would like to thank the following for permission to reproduce photographs:
Alamy p. 9 (Andy Levin); Bridgeman Art Library/© Museum of Fine Arts, Boston, Massachusetts p. 11; Bridgeman Art Library City Art Museum, St. Louis, MO, USA p. 14; Corbis p. 21, pp. 6, 16, 18 (Bettman), 27 (Bruce Burkhardt), 25 (Joseph Sohm; ChromoSohm Inc.), 7 (Owen Franken), 19 (Sean Sexton Collection), 24 (William Manning); Getty Images pp. 10 (Hulton Archive), 15 (National Geographic), 20 (Time & Life Pictures); Jill Birschbach/Harcourt Education Ltd pp. 4, 5, 22, 23, 28, 29; Library of Congress p. 8; Monticello/Thomas Jefferson Foundation, Inc. p. 17; Peter Newark's Americana Pictures pp. 12–13.

Cover photograph of the Thomas Jefferson Memorial reproduced with permission of Lonely Planet Images.

In recognition of the National Park Service Rangers who are always present at the memorials, offering general information and interpretative tours. We thank you!

Every effort has been made to contact copyright holders of any material reproduced in this book. Any omissions will be rectified in subsequent printings if notice is given to the publishers.

The publishers and authors have done their best to ensure the accuracy and currency of all the information in this book, however, they can accept no responsibility for any loss, injury, or inconvenience sustained as a result of information or advice contained in the book.

Some words are shown in bold, **like this**. You can find out what they mean by looking in the glossary.

Contents

The Thomas Jefferson Memorial

The Thomas Jefferson **Memorial** is in Washington, D.C., near the Potomac River. It is a white building with a round **dome** and tall **columns**.

4

This memorial honors Thomas Jefferson, the third **president** of the United States. His ideas helped form the government that we still have today.

Founding Father

The early American **colonists** were unhappy with British rule. They asked Thomas Jefferson to help. He was one of the group of men who wrote the **Declaration of Independence**.

The Declaration said that the United States was a free country. The people would make their own laws. Thomas Jefferson was a **founding father** of the United States of America.

A Man of Thought

Thomas Jefferson had many ideas about **freedom**. He believed that all people had the right to life, liberty, and happiness.

Jefferson wanted a government that would not tell anyone what to say or do. He thought people should be free to belong to any **religion**.

Thomas Jefferson spent much of his life serving his country. In 1779, he was **elected** governor of Virginia. Later he became the U.S. **secretary of state**.

In 1797 John Adams became the second **president** of the United States. Jefferson served as his vice president. Four years later Thomas Jefferson became president.

President Jefferson

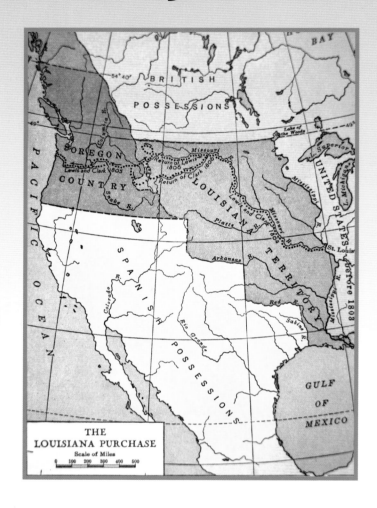

THE
LOUISIANA PURCHASE
Scale of Miles
0   100   200   300   400   500

President Thomas Jefferson wanted the
United States to grow. In 1803 he bought the
land called the Louisiana Purchase
from France.

President Jefferson sent Meriwether Lewis and William Clark west to find a waterway across the United States. He also told them to collect samples of new plants and animals.

Leader in Education

Thomas Jefferson knew that a strong and free country needed educated **citizens**. He helped plan free schools for all of the students in Virginia.

Jefferson was the founder of the **University** of Virginia. He helped find teachers and books. It was one of the first state universities in the United States.

The Farms at Monticello

Thomas Jefferson designed and built a home on a hilltop in Virginia. He planted **orchards** and crops across his land. He also kept animals.

16

Jefferson chose the name Monticello for his home and farms. This was his favorite place to be. Thomas Jefferson died at Monticello on July 4, 1826.

Planning a Memorial

In 1934 the U.S. Congress asked a **commission** to plan and build a **memorial** for **President** Jefferson in Washington, D.C. They asked John Russell Pope to **design** it.

He planned the same style of building that Jefferson used for his home at Monticello. It looked like the Pantheon, an ancient church in Rome.

Saving Cherry Trees

Not everyone liked the **memorial** plan. Many cherry trees would be cut down. A few people chained themselves to trees to save them.

The builders listened to the people. More cherry trees were planted than were cut down. Then people were happy with the site for the memorial.

Building the Jefferson Memorial

Workers used white **marble** to build the walls and 54 **columns** for the **memorial**. They put a **bronze** statue of Thomas Jefferson in the center.

22

This statue stands tall and looks out toward the White House. The memorial was **dedicated** on April 13, 1943. This would have been Jefferson's 200th birthday.

Remembering Thomas Jefferson

At the Thomas Jefferson **Memorial** we remember a great man and **president**. This **sculpture** of the people who wrote the **Declaration of Independence** shows him as a **statesman**.

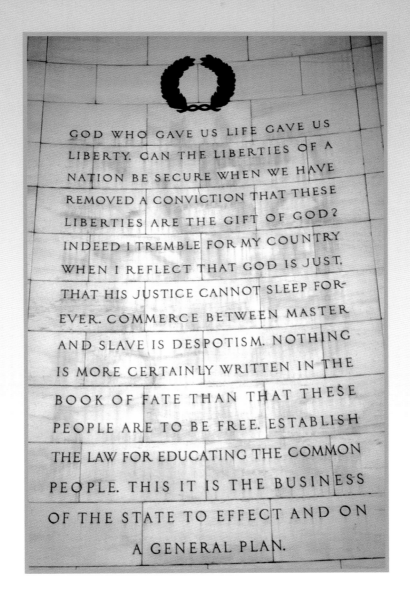

GOD WHO GAVE US LIFE GAVE US LIBERTY. CAN THE LIBERTIES OF A NATION BE SECURE WHEN WE HAVE REMOVED A CONVICTION THAT THESE LIBERTIES ARE THE GIFT OF GOD? INDEED I TREMBLE FOR MY COUNTRY WHEN I REFLECT THAT GOD IS JUST, THAT HIS JUSTICE CANNOT SLEEP FOR-EVER. COMMERCE BETWEEN MASTER AND SLAVE IS DESPOTISM. NOTHING IS MORE CERTAINLY WRITTEN IN THE BOOK OF FATE THAN THAT THESE PEOPLE ARE TO BE FREE. ESTABLISH THE LAW FOR EDUCATING THE COMMON PEOPLE. THIS IT IS THE BUSINESS OF THE STATE TO EFFECT AND ON A GENERAL PLAN.

Jefferson's words are carved on the walls. They remind us that he was a great thinker and writer. His writings about **freedom** are still important today.

Visiting the Thomas Jefferson Memorial

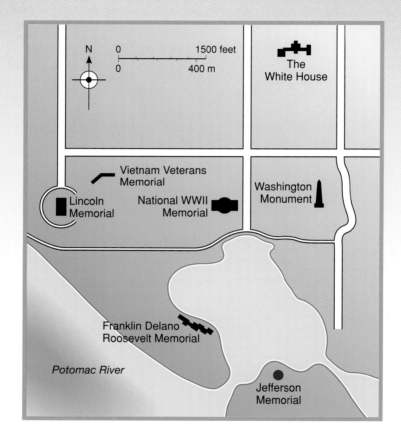

Here is a map of the **National Mall** showing the Jefferson **Memorial**. When you visit read the famous words of Thomas Jefferson on the inside walls.

This memorial reminds us of Thomas Jefferson and his ideas. He helped bring **freedom** of speech and **religion** to Americans.

Fact File

Thomas Jefferson Memorial

★ The Thomas Jefferson **Memorial** weighs about as much as 5,800 African elephants. Now that's heavy!!

★ The bronze statue of Thomas Jefferson inside the memorial stands very tall. If three people stood on top of each other it would be almost the same height.

★ Thomas Jefferson died on July 4, 1826. This day was exactly 50 years after the **Declaration of Independence** was adopted.

★ Thomas Jefferson's picture is on the front of the nickel. His home at Monticello is on the other side. This is another way that Americans remember this important man.

Timeline

Thomas Jefferson Memorial

★ 1743   Thomas Jefferson is born in Virginia

★ 1769   Jefferson begins building at Monticello

★ 1776   Jefferson and others write the **Declaration of Independence**

★ 1801–1809   Jefferson is **president** of the United States

★ 1826   Jefferson dies at Monticello

★ 1934   U.S. Congress sets up a Thomas Jefferson Memorial **Commission**

★ 1937   The site for the Thomas Jefferson Memorial is chosen

★ 1939   President Franklin D. Roosevelt lays the cornerstone and building work starts

★ 1943   The Thomas Jefferson Memorial is finished and **dedicated**

Glossary

bronze hard, reddish brown metal that is a mixture of copper and tin

citizen resident of (living in) a particular city or country

colonist someone who lives in a colony – an area or country ruled by another country

column tall, upright pillar that helps hold up a building or statue

commission group of people who meet to do a certain task or job

Declaration of Independence written announcement that the thirteen American colonies were free from British rule

dedicate have a ceremony that opens a new bridge, hospital, or memorial

dome rounded top of a building that looks like half of a ball

elect choose someone or decide something by voting

founding fathers men who talked about and wrote the first documents of the United States government, such as the Declaration of Independence and the Constitution

freedom having the right to say, behave, or move around as you please

marble hard, white stone used to make buildings and statues

memorial something that is built to help people remember a person or an event

National Mall large, park-like area of land in Washington, D.C. where museums and memorials are built

orchard field or farm where fruit trees are grown

president person chosen by the people of a republic as their leader

religion particular system of belief or worship

sculpture something carved or shaped out of stone, wood, metal, marble, or clay

secretary of state person who talks on behalf of a country to other countries

statesman leader who works to do good for the people

university school that people can go to after high school to do more study

More Books to Read

An older reader can help you with these books:

Ansary, Mir Tamin. *Presidents' Day*. Des Plaines, Ill.:
  Heinemann Library, 1999.

DeGezelle, Terri. *The Thomas Jefferson Memorial*. Mankato, Minn.:
  Capstone Press, 2004.

Ferry, Joseph. *The Jefferson Memorial*. Philadelphia, Pa.:
  Mason Crest, 2003.

Visiting the Memorial

The Thomas Jefferson Memorial is open every day of the year, except Christmas Day (December 25), 8:30 A.M. to 11:45 P.M. Park rangers are present during these times to answer questions or give talks on the memorial.

To ask for a brochure and map of the Thomas Jefferson Memorial, write to this address:

National Park Service
900 Ohio Drive SW
Washington, D.C. 20024.

Index